By

DR ARPITA SINGH

DEDICATED
FOR
GOOD HEALTH

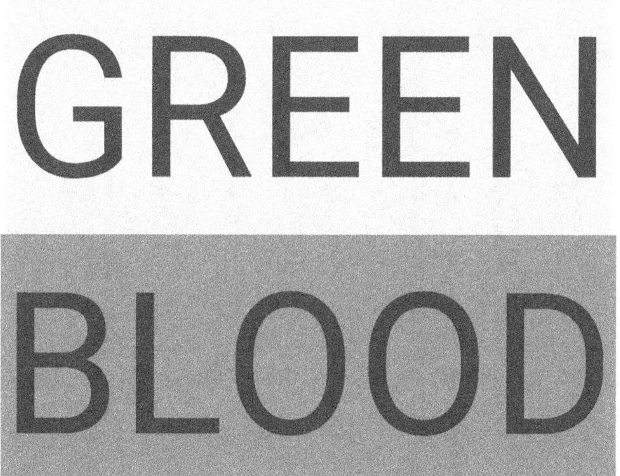

CONTENTS

A. What is GREEN ████████ ?

★ Wheat grass juice is known as Green blood as it bears a closer resemblance to the haemoglobin found in human blood.

★ Chemically, human blood and wheat grass are very similar in constitution. The constitution of human blood is a bit alkaline. It stays in a very narrow pH range 7.35-7.45. Below or above this range means a disease. If blood pH moves to much below 6.8 or above 7.8, cells stop functioning and the patient dies. The ideal pH for human blood is 7.4. Similarly, wheat grass is also alkaline with the same pH 7.4. This is the reason why wheat grass is quickly absorbed in the blood proving highly beneficial for us.

★ Human blood contains Hemin having iron in the molecule whereas wheat grass contains chlorophyll having magnesium in the molecule. This is the only difference between them.

★ Magnesium found in the chlorophyll molecule is essential and beneficial for about 30 enzymes of our body. Thus, the wheat grass juice was given the name "GREEN BLOOD" by Dr Ann Wigmore.

B. Need of GREEN ██████

1. Are you disgusted with medicines? Are you apprehensive of their side effects?
2. Has your disease persisted inspite of taking a number of medicines?
3. Do you want to provide your body with all essential vitamins and minerals in their natural & live form?
4. Do you wish to remain healthy for long?

Then Resort to Green blood.

★ GREEN BLOOD enhances the natural resistance power of the body against diseases.

★ Take GREEN BLOOD just for 3 weeks. Your diseases will disappear under the powerful curative influence of wheat grass.

★ Your body will be filled with new vigour, your eyes will shine with lustre, your cheeks will show a rosy tinge and your skin will exude youth.

C. GREEN Therapy & diseases?

A list of some of the dreadful diseases in which GREEN BLOOD THERAPY has been found to be an effective remedy.

1. Diseases of the heart & blood circulatory system:

   (a) Anaemia   (b) High blood pressure

   (c) Atherosclerosis   (d) Internal Haemorrhage

2. Diseases of the respiratory system:

   (a) Common cold   (b) Asthma   (c) Bronchitis

3. Diseases of the digestive system:

   (a) Constipation   (b) Indigestion & Flatulence

   (c) Nausea & Vomitting   (d) Acidity

(e) Ulcers in the stomach & intestines

(f) Swelling in the intestines (g) Diabetes

(h) Swelling & pain in the throat (i) Worms

4. Complaints of teeth & gums:

(a) Carries in the teeth   (b) loose teeth

(c) Septic in the gums   (d) Ulceration in the gums (e) Bleeding gums

5. Diseases of the joints:

(a) Swelling in joints (b) Pain in joints

(c) Osteoarthritis   (d) Bone rotting

6. Diseases of the brain & nervous system:

(a) Muscular tremor   (b) Parkinson's disease

7. Skin diseases:

(a) Eczema (b) Acne (Pimples) (c) Boils

(d) Cuts & wounds   (e) Bites   (f) Burns

8. Renal diseases:

(a) Stone   (b) Inflammation of kidneys

(c) Inflammation of the Urinary bladder

9. Diseases of the reproductive system:

(a) Dysmenorrhea or dysmenorrhoea means

painful menstruation, typically involving abdominal cramps.

(b) Sexual debility

10. Ear diseases:

(a) Ear pain (b) Septic discharge from the ear

11. Cancer:

Each and every cancer patient must invariably try this therapy to get rid of this deadly disease.

12. Some other diseases:

(a) General weakness (b) Insomnia

(c) Headache   &   (d) Fever, etc.

D. How to grow WHEAT GRASS?

The beautiful thing about GREEN BLOOD is that it can be obtained by growing wheat grass at home.

Pot selection:

★ The first step to grow wheat grass is to prepare soil bed in your garden if you have enough space there.

★ Wheat grass can be grown in different pots also, if you don't have enough space in your garden.

★ For this purpose, very big or deep pots are not required. Take 7 pots of area 1 square feet, having a depth of about 3 inches.

★ Only 7 pots are needed because wheat grass attains desired height after 7 days.

★ Other items which can be used as a substitute of pots are wooden boxes, lower half of Earthen pots, baskets, big tins or any other suitable container as shown ahead:

Soil, manure & pesticide

★ Any type of soil except very sticky can be used to grow wheat grass.

★ Prepare soil by mixing organic manure, viz., cow-dung & cow-urine, etc.

★ Cow-urine can be used as pesticide also.

★ Chemical fertilizers should never be used.

Wheat quality

★ To get adequate amount of wheat grass juice, we need to sow good quality wheat. Wheat grass grown out of big grains is always broad and full of juice.

Sowing of wheat grains

★ To get 100 g wheat grass, we need to sow 100 g wheat at a time. 100 g wheat grass gives approximately 120-180 ml green blood which is sufficient for one day for a patient. Prepare one pot everyday as follows:

(a) Spread the sprouted wheat grains closely on the soil bed. To sprout the wheat grains, first soak them in water for about 12 hrs. Then wrap them in a wet thick cotton cloth and tie them tightly for another 12-14 hrs.

(b) Cover the grains with a thin layer of soil.

(c) Sprinkle some water over it (not to be poured).

(d) To get better yield mix a few drops of cow-urine with water to be sprinkled.

(e) When the wheat grass grows a bit high, give water only once in 24 hrs in late afternoon or in early evening.

(f) In summers, avoid Sunlight for more than 3-4 hrs and sprinkle water 2-3 times per day.

(g) It is necessary to protect the growing, fresh & tender wheat grass from insects, birds & rodents. A few drops of Cow-urine mixed with water works as a good pesticide.

Left blank for important points to be noted by reader.

E. How to get GREEN ███████ ?

Cutting of Wheat Grass

1. On the 8th day of sowing wheat grains, wheat grass with about 4-5 inches height is ready for cut.

2. Cut it as close to the bottom as possible, with a pair of scissors.

3. If the length of wheat grass is more than 4-5 inches, it has lesser amout of juice.

4. After cutting the grass, the soil in the pot must be spread over in the Sun.

5. This dried soil can be used after about 4-5 days. Mix some fresh soil and organic manure in it before its reuse.

Extraction of Green blood

1. Wash wheat grass properly.

2. Cut it, add some water & crush the fresh wheat grass.

3. Crushing can be done in an electric juicer / mixer or by a manual stone crusher (sil).

4. Strain the juice out of it.

5. GREEN BLOOD is ready for consumption.

F. Proper dosage of GREEN

(a) In an ordinary sickness or for a common ailment, 100 ml juice per day is must. Keep the dosage low in the beginning, increasing it gradually.

(b) In some serious / chronic disease, start with 25-50 ml juice per day and raise it gradually to reach a quantity of 250-300 per day.

(c) For a normal healthy person, 50 ml juice per day is ok.

It is very essential that the wheat grass juice must be taken fresh, soon after it is extracted. The vital elements contained in it start perishing with time thus reducing the efficacy of the GREEN BLOOD.

G. Proper timings for taking GREEN ▮

(a) Take the juice early in the morning or during the day on an empty stomach for best results.

(b) After having wheat grass or Green blood, do not eat or drink any other thing for about half an hour.

(c) You can chew the wheat grass at any convenient time or at short convenient intervals during the day.

H. GREEN ███ nutritional analysis

Test results from

Irvine Analytical Laboratories, Inc.

(Now Irvine Pharmaceutical Services),CA

(*Taken from www.dynamicgreens.com*)

Per 100 gram of Wheat grass contains:

Ash 0.48g, calories 21cal, carbohydrates 2g, chlorophyll 42.2 mg, dietary fiber <0.1g, fat 0.06g, moisture 95g, Protein-N×6.25   1.95g,

VITAMINS: Biotin 10mcg, choline 92.4mg, folic acid/folacin 29mcg, Inositol <0.1g/100g, vitA 427IU, B1 0.08mg, B2 0.13mg, B3 0.11mg, B5 6mg, B6 0.2mg, B12 <1mcg, C 3.65mg, E 15.2IU

MINERALS: Calcium 24.2mg, Iron 0.61mg, Magnesium 24mg, Phosphorous 75.2mg, Potassium 147mg, Selenium <1ppm, Sodium 10.3mg, Zinc

0.33mg

AMINO ACIDS: Alanine 306mg, Aspartic acid 260mg, Cysteine 31.2mg, Isoleucine 56.6mg, L-Arginine 135mg, L-Lysine 37mg, Leucine 105.3 mg, Methionine 93.6mg, Phenylalanine 103.4mg, Proline 237mg, Threonine 280mg, Tyrosine 62.4mg, Valine 44.9mg

ESSENTIAL FATTY ACIDS: Lecithin,food <0.3g, monounsaturated fatty acid <0.1g/100g, polyunsaturated fatty acid <0.1g/100g, saturated fatty acid <0.1g/100g

CARBOHYDRATES: Fructose <0.1/100g, Glucose 0.8g, Lactose <0.1/100g, Maltose <0.1/100g, Sucrose <0.1/100g.

Before employing any other form of treatment, give GREEN BLOOD THERAPY a chance to cure and keep you healthy.

Books in HINDI

1. Hasta-mudra Chikitsa Vigyan

   (ebook in Hindi)

2. Hasta mudra Chikitsa Vigyan

   (Paperback edition in Hindi, B/W),

3. Hasta mudra Chikitsa Vigyan

   (Paperback edition in Hindi, Full color),

Books in ENGLISH

4. CONSTIPATION - Truthful experiments for health

   (ebook in English)

5. KNEE PAIN (Part I) - Truthful experiments for health

   (ebook in English)

6. KNEE PAIN (Part II) - Truthful experiments for health

(ebook in English)

7. HASTA MUDRA YOGA For EMERGENCY RELIEF

(ebook in English)

8. FINGER YOGA

(ebook in English)